Frozen Falls

Akron Series in Poetry

Also by Barry Seiler

Retaining Wall

The Waters of Forgetting

Black Leaf

Akron Series in Poetry

Elton Glaser, Editor

Barry Seiler, *The Waters of Forgetting*
Raeburn Miller, *The Comma After Love: Selected Poems of Raeburn Miller*
William Greenway, *How the Dead Bury the Dead*
Jon Davis, *Scrimmage of Appetite*
Anita Feng, *Internal Strategies*
Susan Yuzna, *Her Slender Dress*
Raeburn Miller, *The Collected Poems of Raeburn Miller*
Clare Rossini, *Winter Morning with Crow*
Barry Seiler, *Black Leaf*
William Greenway, *Simmer Dim*
Jeanne E. Clark, *Ohio Blue Tips*
Beckian Fritz Goldberg, *Never Be the Horse*
Marlys West, *Notes for a Late-Blooming Martyr*
Dennis Hinrichsen, *Detail from* The Garden of Earthly Delights
Susan Yuzna, *Pale Bird, Spouting Fire*
John Minczeski, *Circle Routes*
Barry Seiler, *Frozen Falls*
Melody Lacina, *Private Hunger*

Barry Seiler

Frozen Falls

The University of Akron Press
Akron, Ohio

Cover photograph by Bob Stewart.

Cover design by Kachergis Book Design.

Acknowledgements:

Some of the poems in this book appeared in the following journals: *Comstock Review, Hanging Loose, The Ledge, Mystic River Review, Patterson Review,* and *WV Magazine.*

An earlier version of this collection received the Capricorn Poetry Award of the Writer's Voice West Side Y.

All inquiries and permission requests should be addressed to the Publisher,
The University of Akron Press, 374B Bierce Library, Akron, Ohio 44325–1703.

LIBRARY OF CONGRESS CATALOGING-IN-PUBLICATION DATA

Seiler, Barry.
Frozen falls : poems / by Barry Seiler.—1st ed.
p. cm. —(Akron series in poetry)
ISBN 1-884836-78-X
I. Series.
PS3569.E535 F76 2001
811′.54–DC21

2001003097

Manufactured in the United States of America

The paper used in this publication meets the minimum requirements of American National Standard for Information Sciences—Permanence of Paper for Printed Library Materials, ANSI Z39.48–1984. ∞

First Edition

For Elton Glaser and Helen Glaser

Contents

III

IV

V

I

Wellwood

This is what they have chosen,
this little village of the departed
cousins and countrymen
not so far out on the Island

where my mother dreamed of retirement—
a woman of property, with a stole,
her children schooled and thriving,
secure in the American elsewhere—

where the Rosenbergs rest in peace,
whom I mistook for my parents,
hiding myself beneath the kitchen table,
a little spy among the limbs.

I've been twice to gather stones
to place on their headstones as signs
that the living recall the departed.
By now they must be overgrown

with weeds and wildflowers, the odd seeds
exiled by migrating birds. I should return
and perform a son's duty.
I've studied the route:

from Penn to Pinelawn Station,
and a quick cab ride to the cemetery.
The driver will wait as I tend
to my business: say the words,

arrange the stones, tidy up.
There is glamour in the waiting cab.
There is glamour in the ticking meter,
an orphan's glamour,

to count out for all to hear
and peel off the bills, to say, casually,
to the indifferent driver the way the big shots do,
Keep the change.

Hat

I've always wanted to wear one,
lifting it by the crown with the palm
of my left hand, off the little table
I placed for it by the door,

snap-brimming it on the way out.
My father wore one every day,
ash-gray, a thick, black ribbon
circling it, a mourner's band,

a touch of elegance to his
otherwise dreary life, binding him
to those other characters born
at the turn of the century: Bogart,

Gable, Gary Cooper, silent
as my old man. What did Hemingway
say about Cooper?
He beat me to the barn door.

I love those empty phrases
spoken out the side of the mouth,
the hat at a jaunty angle,
a dash of bravado. I can see myself

like George Raft near the end:
ducking the tax raps, small-talking
the high rollers and their ladies,
flipping that coin, a little bored,

a little amused to have come to this,
winking as they enter, winking again
as they exit, tipping my hat
like a stagedoor Johnny.

Mercy Stick

Did your father ever stop and say: *Son,*
don't take the short end of the mercy stick?
Perhaps he was standing at the bedroom door,
getting ready for the next day's shift,
examining the scuff marks on his shoes
the way seers examine feces,
seeking the future in the old day's waste.
And you could see something pliant, a switch,
and wondered whether mercy was the stick
itself, or the hand that lifts and swiftly falls.

The Green Book

Who placed it on the shelf surrounded by
Uris, Wouk, and *The Rise and Fall of the Third Reich?*
Dried and flaking, the pages smelled like trash
left out overnight in the rain,
its green skin wrinkled and faded
like the crumpled dollar bills my father pulled
from his pocket and left on the dresser.
What was it? Some thick slice of Shakespeare?
The poems of Alfred Lord Tennyson?
Tolstoi or Milton abandoned by a happier family?
Memory returns only the double columns,
twin waterfalls of words that poured down the page,
the sources mysterious to me as the sources of the Nile.

On a Long Strand of Hair Found in a Biography of Frank O'Hara

She bows her head above the book,
sitting on the wicker on the screened-in porch
facing the Sound. She's skimming,
eager to get to the early sixties scene,
the frantic mountings and couplings.
Later she examines the webs tattooed along her thighs,
peeking over her shoulder like a pinup girl.
Poems live in those places where furniture
and flesh meet. There in the burn and fade.
After lunch, she carries a basket to the shore
and stretches out and reads until she drifts to sleep,
light enough to hear the wind moving its lips
across the pages. Evening, he drives back from the City.
Tie askew, drink in hand, he gossips about the gallery.
She describes the odd trajectory of the career:
the booze, the lovers, the politics of Art.
Art, she says with a capital A.
She says: *The days go by so goddamned quickly*
when you're here on your own. But then, you know,
you reach an hour late afternoon
that simply will not budge. The sun just hangs there,
flummoxed, unsure of its instructions.
That's nice, he says, meaning the way the sun sets
highlights in her hair. *It looks professional.*
A cool breeze slips through the window
and two mosquitoes blow into the room,
shifting the weight of evening toward autumn.
Well, he says, for no clear reason, *that's all she wrote.*

And the hair falls. Or had fallen earlier,
pages tossed over it like spadefuls of earth.
She rises and rubs the back of her neck
and feels the slight swell and curses softly.
She pours a nightcap to carry up with the book.
As she ascends, she turns. *Wasn't it all*
just a little too full, she says,
balancing book and drink on the banister,
twisting her hair into a chignon. *I know*
how it ends, she says, *but I'll read on anyway.*

Poem with Two Lemons

Here are two lemons for your poem,
two sour souls in exile, eking out a living.
What do they see, fresh off the boat,
with their wide-eyed appraising gaze?

We have come very far to deliver them,
traveling by night like undocumented aliens.
Shall we place them on the kitchen table?
We only want to do for you.

What do you see? Two bright refusals,
two thick-skinned naysayers?
Moonlight pouring through a high window
molds a bowl for you. Dust motes

rise toward the light: a ladder,
a tongue, whatever you want.
When the dust settles down, do they resemble
two veiled widows on a mourning bench,

their husbands dead in the Great War?
We can give you their corpses, face up,
unblinking, toward the sun.
Who might have arranged them so,

two parallel lines reaching for the horizon?
Was it someone with a sense of occasion,
or did chance place them so?
Do you suppose one man is your grandfather

on your mother's side, your namesake?
Do you suppose he ever put
a wedge of lemon next to a glass of tea,
both atop a milk-white saucer,

all glowing with the mysteries of placement?
Do you suppose he ever squeezed the lemon
into the glass and watched a few seeds
float slowly to the bottom,

and from his forefinger licked a drop of juice
and made a face from bitterness,
and his mouth puckered into a bemused *No?*
This might have been 1906.

In the next room, his wife and infant daughter
slept. Do you suppose he thought,
a man could do worse than this,
these few minutes' peace in the kitchen?

Do you suppose he picked the glass up
with his thumb and forefinger
and studied it in the lantern light?
Did he think a glass, after all,

is merely a glass? Or did he hold it
as close to his ear as the heat permitted,
believing everything in God's creation
aches with longing to explain itself?

And did he laugh, finally, a man alone
in his kitchen behaving foolishly,
and quickly sip the scalding tea,
his mouth alive with lemon, lemon?

A Dream of My Father Reading

I'm back at my first address,
seeing this for the first time.
My father sits on the living room sofa,
reading a book of my poems.

A skullcap of light burns through the window
over his shoulder, illuminating the pages.
I'm there, too, the child in the corner
against the wall, watching,

trying to take the measure of the man.
My father never reads a book.
He slices their pages for a living, binds
and releases them into the air like homing pigeons,

bound beyond the borders of his caring.
Each evening, he washes off any trace of print
in the kitchen sink, any anger risen from his skin,
any desire. What does he see in mine?

The book is large, coffee-table size,
a shirt of poems covering his frail chest.
The title is *Furnishings,* his title,
the title of a practical man, well-versed

in making something of something else
and coming home to the certainties
of table and chair, a firm mattress
for his aching back. As he reads,

he nods, shaking his head up and down,
a trace of prayer in his movement.
He pushes his glasses up the bridge of his nose,
a quick move, like the wind of his Benrus watch

each morning he rises and shines across the city.
I see his spectral body tremble. What have I written
that moves him so? Day breaks in my room.
Yes, he whispers. Yes to what I write.

Waking, I'm released to my father's approval.

II

❄

Lamp

It's no easy life
patrolling the frontier between the dark out there
and the dark in here.

Out there,
your counterpart stares at the ground,
clanking in place, bowing his head modestly
to his lady love.

He seems so cold out there,
his slender body trembling,
his throat humming
the lonely tune of the empowered.

Perhaps you should call a truce
in the bitter war between inside and outside,
traverse the no-man's land, stand shoulder to shoulder—
comrades, however briefly.

Light this house from the outside in.

Dust

There, under your bed,
those little Hasids reel deliriously,
beards and forelocks flapping.

Such ecstasy in such restrictions!

They've been singing all day.
Their throats are as parched as the Promised Land
they dream of entering.

Someday they will gather up their belongings
and pack them in cardboard suitcases
and, little band of brothers, cross over,
swift as a pencil erasing.

And where will you be then,
you with your nose in the air,
you sitting on the edge of the bed,
waiting for the other shoe to fall?

Clock (1)

What is it about birds and clocks?

What is it about the owl's hoot,
the bluejay's chatter on the hour,
that has to do with the sadness of time passing?

What is it about the moron
tossing it from the roof,
wanting to see time fly?

What is it about the cuckoo's catchy tune,
the over and over of it,
that eases the awful weight of time?

Beds and Doors

Who made the decision
to separate the bed from the door?

Where was it written?

Sundered at birth, they pine for each other
across the vast chasm of the house.

You can hear them call to each other
in the high-pitched plaintive voice
the not-quite-living use.

How's by you? it sounds like.

How's by you?

Armchair (1)

Whipped beast of the domestic life.

Take it.
Take it and take it and take it.

Until the last straw.
Until the final body eases down and sighs.

Until it rises and walks away,
leaving nothing, crumbs and coins,
a shadow of itself.

And then you will rise, unburdened,
seeing for the first time that small burn,
delicate as a beauty mark,
on your soft, indentured flesh.

Table

We were mistaken—
the table does have an inner life,
filled as ours with anger and desire.

The one in the bedroom fancies itself a wall
of cool white plaster.
It wishes to stand upright in the world,
to feel flesh pressed to flesh.

The one in the parlor dreams of a mighty flood
washing this town away.
It dreams of being carried out to sea,
free of its cleverly arranged burdens.

It dreams of being open to anything,
like the lifted lid of an ornate coffin.

Dishes

Here we live to eat and they to serve.
And we meet at the table, assuming our positions.

And when we are done,
when they are nicked, cracked,
their familiar patterns gone strange,
revealed beneath the roast, the good stew;

when they no longer amuse us
as they arrive at the table
heaped with our steaming portions;
when we no longer rise sated
from what we devour—
what then, my friend, what then?

Will we pass them on,
fragile tokens of how well we lived,
how tastefully?

Or will the great trucks lift them,
those tender morsels,
roughly, to their maws?

The Sink's Story

Long ago the sink was a mirror,
but its appetite for the body was insatiable.

You know how the story goes.
The mirror wept inconsolably
until, taking pity on it,
the gods turned it into a spring.

Well, a passing herdsman came upon it
and, enchanted by the running water,
fell in love with his face rippling in it.
And so on. And so on.

As you know, to this day
the sink, out of its deep well of gratitude,
will gladly swallow anything to please you—
all those snippets of self
the body in its mortal discontent
disdains.

Stairs

Before we were stairs, we were roads.
You could travel us to the edges of the empire
and gawk as you pleased at the natives.

If you doubt us, consider this little pebble
nesting in the carpet. Each morning,
you step on it as you make your journey
to your morning coffee.

How did it arrive at the fourth step?
Did it finally surrender to exhaustion,
limping ahead of an invading army?

That low throbbing in your heel, that blister,
is the pebble singing its tragic tale.
It was told at birth it would go far in the world.
It was told it would be substantial.
But it was misled.

Before we were roads, my friend,
trust us, we were riverbeds.

Clock (2)

The big hand plays the good cop,
the little hand the bad.

The big hand straightens his tie in the mirror,
spit-slicks his hair,
winks at himself in the two-way glass
as if he has all the time in the world.

The little one smacks his nightstick against your armrest.
It vibrates down to the balls of your feet
and back up again. You shake
like a cartoon pig on a window ledge.

I'm gonna ask you this just once, he barks.
Once, once, once.

When the light shrinks as if it's been through the wash,
he slaps cold water on your face
from one of those little cups shaped like a dunce cap.

You know the kind we mean—
the kind these guys like to crush in their fists
and, eyes shut tight, shoot at the trash.

Desk

Little boat at anchor—
we have waited so long for the natives to row out
with their breadfruit.

When will their drums at long last cease?
What strangeness will we taste?

Through my spyglass, I see the native girls
swaying in their skirts of flowers.
They tell a story with their hands!

Dearest,
the wind has not stirred for days.
I take pen in hand to write,
for I fear we will not see home.

Vase

From your throne on the kitchen table,
you survey your little domain.

The smaller the realm,
the more brutal the rule.

Allow me to place this pink tongue
in your always displeased mouth.
Now you may address your subjects
on pressing matters of state.

And so you will reign undisturbed
until that day the pinched winter sun
throws down its black glove.

Armchair (2)

To exist as a permanent shrug.
To hold and let go, hold and let go.

To keep only the trace of the thing,
the way an eraser keeps the dust of the word.

In memoriam,
like ashes in an urn.

Curtains

The scattered applause of the maple leaves.
And then it's curtains, curtains.

Blue tongue. Blue tongue.
Can either of you say where the past belongs?

Here, on the inside,
or on the outside looking in?

III

The Skeleton's Longing

A skeleton walks into a bar
(stop me if you've heard this one before)
and asks the bartender for a beer
and a bucket. All the patrons laugh.
We all love a clever sight gag.
The skeleton unscrews his shinbones
and plays his ribcage like a xylophone.
Unchained Melody, Cry Me a River
pour forth in a tumult of longing.
Everything in the bar goes still,
except for that steady dripping.

My Father Accepts Delivery

To the wrong address. The delivery men curse,
trying to angle the mattress in,
pausing to wipe the sweat, calculating.
My father stands to the side.
Not asked for help, he offers none.
We sit in my parents' bedroom
on my parents' bed, paralyzed,
appalled at the error.
I tell you I will go to the door soon.
Give me a moment. Let me compose myself.
I will tell them they are making a terrible mistake.
Rest assured, I say. But I don't move,
though we must have a home of our own.

Some Falls in Winter

Stepping from the Erie
Lackawanna into a back-
lash of sunlight, dizzy

and mortal, I lost my grip
and saw my left foot
caught in the gap, twisted,

falling, falling forward
to the stone platform.
The blood thin and pink,

old man's blood
trickling from my scalp.
I touched the little pool,

damp, drying into stone,
going away.
My own stunned fingers

touched that blood.
How large my body felt
among strangers, wishing

to rise, desiring grace,
to toddle off, little engine,
under its own steam.

Walking to work, I thought
of Montgomery Clift
falling flat on his face

in Terminal Station; the abyss
between desire and our names
for it opens, and we stare

into our own unblinking
final faces. How beautiful
was that face before the ravages,

before the accidents left him
damaged goods—nerves
barely bundled under the skin—

and the camera looked away,
and the gods looked away,
and we looked and looked away

toward our own affairs.
And he spiraled downward through the lens
toward early death.

I limped along, my knee skinned and shining
quite brilliantly through my pants.
It hurt to the touch, and I

desired comfort, those ancient lips
to taste and heal, a rose of spit
to bloom inside the wound.

American Misfortune

Let's agree you have been blessed.
You have a loving husband
who brings home his paycheck.
He doesn't drink it away.
He doesn't play the ponies.
Let's agree you have two children,
a girl and boy, ages six and ten,
loving, never at a loss,
like those wise children
on the screen, perfectly lit,
plausibly normal. Soon
you will consider attending college
to earn a degree in accounting,
specializing in taxes,
and to raise the level of your self-esteem,
eventually bringing home a second income
to ease the household burdens.
It is a quiet life, as you prefer,
but deeply lived in the pleasures
of similar days, on the grid
of the local, safe between
the many and the one, and sound,
we say, as a dollar bill.

❄

Or here is another story we can tell you,
drawn from the undiminished text.
One day your husband feels a pain
deep in his abdomen.

He lays down his tools,
picks up his lunch pail,
and comes home early from work.
Honey, it's like a rock,
like I don't know what.
Like I swallowed a lobster whole
and it's crawling around in there
like my stomach is the bottom of the sea.
The pain comes and goes.
You can chart its rise and fall
like a stock you have bet the nest egg on.
Finally, it grips down for keeps.
For a long time, the doctors can't
get a handle on it. And you think:
That's the worst part, the not knowing,
the not having a word for it
you can pass back and forth
across the table like sugar,
through the intersections
of the evening's traffic. How bad
can it be if they have no name for it?
And then they do.

❄

Is it misfortune then to tend him
at home on a little bed
you've made from a couch,
to hush the children,
curse the telemarketers?
Is it misfortune to work
in a diner on Route 17,
to come home through

the unnerving evening rush?
Is it misfortune to devote
yourself to another's misfortune?
After, you wed again another decent man—
Who gets that lucky twice?
You feel a diminished, steady love,
more than enough to make a life,
though not the life you bargained for.
You bear another child,
a son to break the tie,
who will carry his name forward
like a blank check
into whatever life he owes the future.

❄

Or is this misfortune?
A friend of the family comes to the door,
a professional, in his middle forties,
divorced, with a young son and daughter.
All night he has been smoking crack
and now needs your support.
Help him, please, get into rehab.
Haven't you been where he is?
Haven't we all been there:
knocked on a door, called
someone in the dead of night,
the package store closed,
the automatic teller empty,
our voices tight with need for others,
angry almost,
as if we were the ones opening the door,
as if we were the ones put upon,

putting intolerable weight on
a simple *please* or *thank you.*

❄

He needs to be outside,
so you lead him out back.
It is a spacious, tree-lined property,
more than an investment,
a place to live your life
and end your days
with a peace you have earned
through regular payment
and accrued interest.
He walks to the edge and peers
across a vast plowed field
intently at a neighbor's house,
as if some irrevocable decision
is being made about him there,
people gathered around a table,
listening to reports, casting votes.
All you see are a few lights
poking through the dark like shoots,
but someone lives there, a family,
sleeping now, unaware, no doubt
with tribulations of their own,
entitled, they feel, to remedies.
And then he walks in circles
thirty feet in circumference, round
and round in a deliberate way,
staring at the ground, chanting
a sequence of numbers,
enacting a ceremony whose meaning
he alone can follow.

And when you ask him what he is doing,
he considers the question
carefully and replies: *I guess*
I'm walking away from myself.

❄

The children live with their mother now
who is a nurse in Florida,
where people in these straits arrive
like driftwood washed up on the shore.
She writes you occasionally.
Nothing much, just small talk,
skittering around the surface of things
in that telegraphic style we employ,
our lovely, evasive vernacular
of loss and gain.
You hear he checked himself into rehab,
is clean now and sober,
regularly attending meetings,
making the necessary confessions
of personal bankruptcy,
beginning to balance the books.
You hear he's married again,
one or two witnesses at City Hall
down by the financial district.
Let's agree she is a woman
with great reserves of forbearance,
who sees qualities in him
worth the investment.

❄

Your husband, his best friend, dies,
hit by a drunken driver

in a quiet suburb of Jersey,
the kind of place where wild turkeys
strut the grassy divide.
He was crossing the street
to get to the other side.
That's all. Just taking a walk
in the evening after a satisfying meal.
Please understand, this is not ironic.
People walk out every day and fail to return,
the ties binding them shredded. Let's agree,
we are all feeling our way,
one way or the other,
trying to find the proper balance
to make it across to the other side,
like tightrope walkers above a falls
or daredevils between twin towers.

❄

After the funeral, people
return to the house and you serve
coffee and cake on the good china:
country castles hovering in the blue,
maidens with milk pails hanging
on their shoulders—any moment
one might stumble and the milk
splash and spill lavishly over blue grass;
shepherds on blue hillsides, one foot
forever raised in forward motion,
piping home the flock. When you
examine them closely, you see
a whole world aching to break
into coherence. As people do

at these times, you sit around
in the living room swapping stories:
humorous stories of loss,
of terrible loss, without rhyme
or reason, quirky stories
of people who run out of luck
and disappear, or just disappear
taking what luck they can bear
and setting up shop elsewhere.
The usual American stories
with the usual endings: flare-ups
or fade-outs, or the quiet goings-on
about our business.

❋

Someone says, for want of something
else to say, he died too young.
How clear life is, someone says,
as tidy as a made-for-TV movie
when you look back on it;
how satisfying at the end when,
arm in arm, the family walks back
to the open door in the glow of the porch light,
and the door slowly closes on us,
and the credits crawl by;
how inevitable those resolutions
once you see the shape of it. How lucky we are,
someone says, to be able to look back
and see the shape and move on
to the next story. And it's true,
you think, we do move on. But where,
and to what end, and what does it amount to?

And you think of the eccentric millionaire
in the old movie of marital mix-up
who keeps a precise record of each purchase.
Even as the mourners speak, you see him
peering owl-like, making another entry
in his little black book. *I write things down,*
he says to the bemused woman
fleeing her befuddled husband
from one screwball circumstance to the next,
pratfalling for love. *I write things down,*
but I don't add them up.

Snow at Night

I can almost say by heart that little poem
by de la Mare about Napoleon in Russia,
in which Napoleon tells his troops

he is the snow and solitude
through which they pass. I can almost
envy the vastness of his vanity.

He calls himself the northern sky.
He himself is the field of battle,
his body, his soul.

I can almost envy the grandeur
he lent those disasters: frozen fingers
unable to grip the bloody sword,

a tattered cloak on a muddy field,
a horse frozen into a lake,
snowflakes winking across its great dark eyes.

All taken into that legendary body
and transformed. Tonight, the snow,
heaps and drifts of it, holds us

where we live, slows down the traffic
on Union Turnpike. I see my neighbor,
overcoat over pajamas,

smoking a cigarette, watching the snow
flare up under his dog's amber piss.
He stands like a god brooding over

a puff of smoke, a stream of urine.
The snow will be radiant, beautiful,
until the soot blooms and the yellow plows

roll down Queens Boulevard,
slashing a path to the Island.
And it will be beautiful

to stand by the window in wild weather,
taking in the army of stoic faces climbing the hill,
returning from their fruitless local wars.

All their lives nothing but lost ground.

Elections

1

Stoned on Keats, we longed for
the dizzying glamour of early death,
a little. How quickly the poems came,

pastiches of the so-so, whose ranks
we desired to swell. *Don't worry,*
our professors assured us,

there's room for us all on Mt. Parnassus.
Eventually, some of us did die.
Some of us fell, with great relief,

into the secular world of work and love,
the small manageable blessings
of door and roof the rest of us pooh-poohed.

Personally, I plodded on,
pursuing what Delmore Schwartz calls
This most fatiguing of occupations,

believing well into middle life
these little poems could make a life,
that they could house our ill spirits.

2

Surprised by a copy of his first chapbook,
a friend punches the glass out of a door,
for joy. He raises his sliced hand in the air

like a bloody banner, shouting:
I'm a poet. I'm a poet. A fucking poet.
Glass and blood dance around the room.

3
November, 1968. Election night.
Moon-faced Humphrey of the pitiful henna,
barely tethered to the platform,

concedes, a glint of cancer in his eye.
Nixon—that puppet pulling his own strings—
lifts his arms to heaven. Before him,

the placards implore: *Now more than ever.*
We pass around wine and joints.
As the precincts report, we spray-paint

graffiti over the candidates' faces,
layer on layer, each in turn,
until only a faint flicker remains,

ghost candidates jitterbugging
back of the blackened screen.
Years later, I get the joke.

In the Catskills

Postwar spring. Early June.
Or is it late summer?
Labor Day? My mother

strains to remember.
I hear this again and again.
She will die soon. Her face

has the clarity of water
running over stone.
Finally: *No matter.*

I am two, and we are in
the Catskills. My mother says:
Summers were better then.

She remembers many white
and yellow flowers, the morning sun
leaping out of the swimming pool,

a shadow doing laps.
My mother says:
We were happier then.

I was a beautiful child,
dark-skinned, and when
I arrived, a full head of hair,

soft and curly, a cherub's locks.
At Grossinger's, strangers in bathing suits
lifted me to the sky, their thin legs

wavering like the long stems
of undersea plants. And I squealed out
my portion of joy. *So much,*

my mother says, *it hurt my ears.*
But I got the whooping cough,
and no one would hold me.

They turned away, my mother says.
I grew silent. I withdrew. *That's why*
you started to stutter, my mother says.

It hurt so much I wanted to speak for you.
I spat out my words to the world,
shattered mirrors. *Everything broken,*

my mother says. *Everything gone.*
We sit in a restaurant picking at
our garden salads. Distracted,

speaking of nothing,
my mother says: *So tell me,*
darling, are you taking care?

Exits

Early bee frisking shrubs on MLK,
doing his *bee-loud* business. I'm hanging
with the smokers, puffing him to

a furious dance outside Hill. Inside,
my students pen their practice Exits,
analyzing "Why Boys Don't Play with Dolls."

I see them bent over their blue books
like Narcissus at the pool.
What beauty can they discern

in their reflections?
What fruit will their labors bear?
Better to dive in, like the foul-mouthed

schoolgirls at Central High across the street.
Aren't they especially fresh today, as light
in the world as bread just lifted from the oven?

The ambulance that sirens by stitches us
into one seamless scene: bee-buzzers, cloud-shifters,
earnest rehearsers for the real world,

blooming fuck you-ers of Newark, New Jersey.

Night People: My Lost Book

When did I write it? Still, it's entered
under my name, call number and all
the pertinent info in the card catalogue.

Perhaps these are my lost years, the ones
that elbow their way into your life
like a parenthesis that refuses to shut,

those awful years on your knees
in some dusty showroom selling lady's shoes.
Back then I must have wandered, in a fever

dream of democracy, the lower slopes
of Mt. Parnassus, where Love and Fame
lash on the talented and the almost-

talented alike, and ambition rests
heavily on the collective brow
like a rumbling storm cloud.

Does anyone here remember my publisher,
a little mimeo outfit out of someone's basement
in Buffalo? When did it go under,

The Press of Unyielding Vanity?

Teacher and Student at the Door

1

Together we walked
down the corridor
to the room where I taught
the underskilled how
to organize their thoughts
into units, how to develop
them with sufficient support,
always keeping in mind
their reader-audience,
always asking themselves
if this flew birdlike down
the street and around
the corner and a stranger
found it, would a stranger
understand? Mornings,
they wrote in-class papers
I later corrected,
making my marginal comments
on their efforts to wrestle those subjects
and verbs to agreement,
marking shaky roads
from pronoun to antecedent,
insisting they must agree,
fencing in their wandering
tenses. And, at the end,
urging them to translate
into tamer English
the untranslatable stories
written on their skin.

2

I understood she was Korean,
a nursing student,
here two years, in her
middle twenties, perhaps.
She mentioned an older man:
A relative? A sponsor?
A lover? She spoke
so softly, so earnestly,
so eager to share an intimacy,
how could I tell her
I could not hear?
When we reached the door,
she could not cross the threshold.
In America, I said,
In America, ladies first.
She smiled, bowing slightly:
In Korea, teacher first.
And so we stood, suspended,
teacher and student at the door,
the class inside, staring out,
enthralled. Until, breaking the spell,
I crossed over.

3

From time to time I saw her
in the coffee shop near
the campus, chatting in Korean
with her friends, laughing softly
and easily, holding a cigarette
European style,
not as I understood her

at the door. Eventually,
she disappeared. Perhaps
she graduated. Perhaps
she transferred. Perhaps
the older man, fearing her
acculturation, insisted, and she,
held in his sway, complied.

4
I tell my students
the little story of the student
and teacher at the door
to illustrate the many
barriers, perceived and not
perceived, between cultures.
I say, how can we ever hope
to know each other
except through literature?
But it comes out earnestly,
like a wish. And we laugh.
And one or two may look
at the door, imagining
the scene, or telling themselves
another story, themselves
at the door desiring entrance.

5
Still, I wish they could see
how she held that cigarette
loosely, slightly tilted
toward the dingy ceiling,
with such unapproachable

sophistication. I keep
coming back to the door,
keep wondering how long
we might have stood had I not
entered the room, keep coming back
to the way she held that cigarette,
leaning into her friends, into that veil
of smoke behind which the story
tells itself to itself in language
too fine to be found in translation.

IV

Shelving

It's finding the proper order I love,
weighing and placing the *it* of them,
making a little story of the task.
I place the skinny volumes together
on the bottom shelves.
I use the old organizing principle:
Misery loves company.
They must find some consolation
standing shoulder to shoulder
in the motley congregation.
They must find some companionship
feeling their neighbor's sour breath
blowing by, knowing their troubles
are at least as bad as yours.
As for the stout ones: Well,
the skinny ones will bear that load.
I place them on the skinny ones' heads.
They seem quite pleased there,
sighing like robber barons
patting their ample bellies,
letting the last loop out
at the end of the vagabond ball.

Sketchbook

Bill—
        Even now I recall my mortification.

We were sitting on a park bench on campus,
like two Baruchs dishing out advice, gratis,
about art, this and that,
when you reached over, grabbed my notebook,
an artist's sketchbook.

Even now I recall the feel of that pimpled black cover,
the pleasure of rubbing it like a magic lamp,
waiting for inspiration.

You turned to a pure blank page,
almost holy to me then, in its whiteness—
I could scarcely violate it—
and scribbled a poem about the moment
you were writing the poem:

lovely coeds strolling by,
marine helicopters gawking overhead.

Even now
I recall how you signed with a flourish,
like an artist signing a dashed-off sketch,

pleased by the way you had broken
and entered. And handed it back.

Ruined now,
                    utterly.

Yours,
          truly.

Error

But
all those years I had misunderstood the song,
hearing it: *Broken at the best places.*

I placed it so
in a poem
I wrote on
the Day of
Atonement.

How many years later
did I finally have it right?
Broke down at the Dead's place.

Dead.

As in Grateful,
                    grateful.

❄

In Ashbery's poem
"Civilization and Its Discontents,"
I misread the first line as:
A people chained to its aura.
When, of course, it should be:
A people chained to aurora.

When
at last it came clear to me, I felt light-
headed with gorgeous certainty,
repeating under my breath this mystery:

Aura.

Aurora.

Aura.

Aurora.

❄

Take *nick of time.*
I never understood it as rescue.
As in:
that black cloud in the distance
resolving to cavalry—
trumpets, banners, etc.

As in:
thank god, the waters are receding.

More like nick,
as in:
a trickle of blood in the shaving mirror,
that red,
rising from someplace deep.

Nick,
as in:
gap,
and what answers our gaze
with gaze.

Turns

The wind whistles
through the mouse bones
on the stone floor of

the church tower,
a little softer in April,
almost a whisper.

Prerecorded hymns
bell out
Amazing Grace.

Above the town,
a flock of notes
gathers and circles:

                    was blind
but now I see.

❄

Tied to a bell,
poor cow,
the body goes

where it will.
But only so far,
so long.

❄

And it is
evening, last wash of light,

the sun still this side of the ridge,
a chill coming on, and frost.

❄

We will die here,
rest together,
as people say,
life's labors done,

gone to our reward
in the boneyard,
among the once
solid citizens.

❄

Four goldfinches
hang on the line

like fresh laundry
flapping in the wind,

our feeder one brief station
on their journey elsewhere.

Named as they are,
they must be Jews

each year repeating
the Diaspora:

exile,
        exile.

The unbearable there,
the unbearable here—

the beautiful,
unbearable wherever.

❄

What Promised Land
do they pine for
in their brief lives?

How do they address
their lord as their heads
bob, and they dance

to maintain their balance,
pinned to nothing?

With hectoring?
With sweetest song?

❄

At the estate sale,
we buy a cow,
a Holstein on wood.

Blue sky. Blue clouds.
Sea green pasture.
Sea green mountains.

Pursed lips of butter-
yellow sunrise.

The basic shades
to color us in
our rustication,

the words *New York*
Holstein scrawled
happily above in

naive black letters.
We'll find a place for
this charming sign,

which must have swung,
at some time gone,
outside a red barn.

We fill our house,
and, in turn, our days
fill up and over-

flow with presence.
Make me an offer,
says the daughter,

too worn-out and
put-out for any
show of sentiment,

wanting only to empty
the house and return
to her own. We do:

Eight dollars for a cow.
Five more for a ladder,
just serviceable. Now

we can reach to change
the bulbs the moths
slam dance against

ecstatically—
sweet soul music
of late April—

longing to enter
our little domain.

❄

Arm's length from the end.
                                        Arm's length from the beginning.

Second of July,
middle day,
my birthday.

Thirty years ago
I thought, where
will I be when

I get here?
And by god,
here I am,

tossing stones at
the chipmunks
devouring sun-

flower seeds
at the feeder.

My arm
has lost a yard or two.

Mourning doves, jays,
grackles, squawk

and scatter over the lawn.
Unintended casualties.

The chipmunk pauses
as a stone missiles by.

and chooses discretion
in the skirmish.

Dull moves
of the long twilight struggle.

❋

The wind clarifies,
                                        and the mountains rise.

I mean, of course,
the clouds lift,
an unveiling.

I'm sipping coffee,
half and half, on
the front porch.

Blue pigs on a mug
dance in a circle,
tail to snout. *Cochon.*

A little steam into
the air, like a locomotive
leaving the station.

❄

Pilgrim robins
in the dew.

Worm knowledge.
Cat knowledge.

Resignations.
Seasonal adjustments.

❄

The mountains,
I say,
the mountains.

As though the word
itself had weight: silver
and the stain of snow.

❄

Morning moon,
pearly and faint.

Morning sun,
throbbing under the mountains.

❄

How does it go?
Spring forward,
fall back?

It's always fall back.
Fall back and regroup.

Fall back
and rise up.

Rise up
so early in the morn.

❄

Cat wants out
but shakes his paw

at that chill
running under the door.

Blue jays squawk:
Justice. Justice.

But it comes out: *Seed.*
Seed.

❄

At fifty, I welcome approaching ends:
the flare of leaves, struck match
across the Catskills. Autumn deepens,

and I feel a last flush of warmth,
a Keatsian light of might-have-beens,
of if-you-wills, of living on

beyond the sweet dream of early death,
the bittersweet of middle life.

❄

And nothing much,
nothing that does not pass
of an evening:

a book of poems—
one of the lesser lights
giving thanks for

the so-it-goes,
the be-that-as-it-may—
I can read without my glasses.

Some made-for-TV movie
of pain and healing
with God's help or

the help of family
or community, walking again,
kicking the habit, surviving,

willing yourself to live,
the human spirit,
of course, triumphant.

❋

Redemption,
                    redemption,
our little birdcry.

And a glass of whiskey
to seal the bargain.

❋

As night settles down,
the cat wants out,
and in, or merely

curls between us,
having his way,
purring on the couch,

into his soft and sacred
self, his pleasure song
of pure nowness.

❋

Wind lifts
and the leaves cast their votes,
and the wind and the leaves
go on.

Wind lifts.
Cat curls back to himself.
Cloud covers moon, and moon
drifts back.

❋

Back of the back field
a little way, the leaves

turning
as the century's end
begins.

And what returns
are seasons, pasts
present beyond redemption,

a handful of bitter pills
washed with poetry.
Each day:

leaf fall
and sun rise.

❄

Snow on the picnic table,
snow on the feeder, the bent

evergreen branch, the wrought-
iron porch rail. I'm wakened

by someone calling my name
once, sharply, from out back.

❄

Thirty years past,
I thought silence,
distance, moroseness

were my patrimony.
And so it seems now,
more or less, and toss

in envy, sour fruit
of petty jealousy,

and blessed,
blessed irony.

❄

Moonlight, snowlight,
three ghost rabbits
scavenging. Morning,

only their tracks,
illegible scrawl
in the snow.

❄

Up Stratton Falls, the falls
are frozen, still, gleaming,
one gate to Paradise,

up from the old Baptist Church,
Shaker-yellow against the dun mountains.
Adjacent to it, the headstones

flare up and die down in
the falling sun. Turning home,
we know the snow crusting the stones

will melt by April, that the stones
pressed hard against all weathers
will stand long after we have fallen.

❄

Across a card of Frost's hard face,
these lines from Becker's book of death:

Of what should a man be properly proud?

❄

Hard January light. Half-birthday
and point of no return.

Under the shed, the chipmunks,
drunk on sunflower seeds, sleep it off.

❄

Mourning doves pace our property
meditating their Sunday sermons,
dressed in their best frock coats, hands folded

behind their backs. I think they will
preach patience from their pulpits, patience,
and take what the ground offers up.

The cat and I eye them,
each according to his passing need,
and turn apart to contemplate the homily.

❄

Something distant sings:
Now.
Now, now.

Or is it: *No?*

Or *Know?*

❄

I'll need at least a score of falls
to sort it out. More, in truth,

until I know those evergreens
ringing our place will not

be crushed beneath the weight
of wind and snow, that this

is not their final springing
back, that they will deepen again

and again our small portion
of shade when we are gone.

V

My Father's Body

My father's body is in me now.
We are two awkward dancers pushed together,
locked in embrace until the song's end.
Since childhood we have hated each other,
danced the wary dance of father and son.
That voice that spun in his head, it spins
now in mine, that monosyllabic song
of wanting to be anywhere but here.
His gestures push their way through mine:
the way his fingers touch his forehead,
part headache, part disbelief,
the way he waves his hand dismissively.
His face claims a place in mine:
that glance of insufficiency,
that sideways glance of disdain.

A Dream Half a Life Away

I was never the one in the blue room
where I knew the old man had died
and the book that he must have written
stood open on the washstand next to
the empty glass. I stood at the window,
watching the light climb down the cathedral
like a thief with a knife in his mouth.
I saw the silver-haired man in uniform,
a chauffeur, I guessed, his white gloves
fidgeting the mirror this way and that,
knotting his tie and shooting his cuffs.
And he glanced up from under hooded lids,
and I thought he saw a woman here,
just risen from a pleasant nap, her long
black hair raveling down to the sill.

To a Poet Dead, Born the Same Year as I

Today at the Strand I found your last living book,
The Widening Spell of the Leaves,
in the dollar bin, that boneyard we all decompose in,

the ring
of a coffee cup staining the lavish praise,

and felt
that tightening in the chest we feel
when one who might have outlived us
falls unexpectedly.

I bought it,

pulled it from the ash bin of our minor histories,
much as I've saved my own,
joking against the vanity of human wishes.

Your gaze fills the front cover,
a little sheepish, a little fisheyed.

Were you uneasy in the middle of your life?
Were you thinking this is what our longing leaves us:
these poems,
these little volumes shelved against the what's-to-come?

Nothing,
you write at the end,
Sweet, sweet nothing.

Small mercy.
Small mercy when we come to it.

The Empty Notebook

Burnt sienna cover
aching to flame,
too beautiful for words,
at least my poor wrong-
handed chicken scratches.
Twenty-five years I've kept it
boxed in the closet, contained,
among the fading mimeos,
the obscure little mags I first
camped in beginning my slow
and dispiriting ascent of Mt. Parnassus.
Once or twice a year, late fall,
early spring, whenever
I need to clean and pare,
I retrieve it. I turn
the pages back to front,
letting the years slip away,
feeling for the language
that will not appear,
the only poem I will ever need.
One day I'll close it one last time.
I'll toss it in the trash,
freeing myself of its weight
and requirement, and some soul
will claim it as his own:
one of the late-night rummagers,
those unacknowledged saints
banging and cursing down the block,
making their collection—

my older brother by my father's first wife,
the one who went mad in the old world
and vanished in the camps.

A Dream of My Father Building

At last my mother has a house,
a small cape on Exeter nearby
the Gardens where the swells live.
And still she is not happy. She wanders
room to room, mouthing complaints
to a nonexistent landlord.
My father discovers tools. He measures
the balance of a hammer in the palm of his hand,
like the scales of justice, and finds it true.
He runs his fingers across the blade
of a saw as if he will thrill it into song.
He decides to build a fence to contain
the wanderlust of his small back yard,
to keep on this side of the line
the lighthearted apple blossoms.
He has never made a thing,
never worked with nail or wood,
never unrolled a tape from here to there
and watched it slither back to its nest.
My mother watches from the kitchen window.
The house she dreamed of is a terrible mistake.
We are not a people of property.
Married to this man twenty-five years,
she has never seen him so alive, so willing,
dancing so eagerly to his appointed task.

The Wonder of God

The wonder of God is within,
like smoke inside a good cigar.

There's no point standing there
staring at it, drawing it under your nose
like salts, taking it in.

You must burn it to have it.
You must expel it.

The clever ones shape it:
the mouth of a cave in the Pyrenees,
morning sun burning the mist
off the mountains;
a stick man tipping his hat hello
as he saunters by;
a bull's-eye.

And at the end hangs the ash,
that elegant little thumbs up,
that epilogue, that wink of the eye.

Waters

I'm beginning to believe I never stood
on the coast of Portugal, that I did not
sleep there in a blue bag and feel
my father's lips brushing mine as he bends
to me, almost crossing the border,
that he did not whisper to my mother:
He's sleeping, only sleeping, let him sleep.
I'm beginning to believe I did not wade
at sunrise into the Sea of Libya
and hear the sheep bleat out to me from the shore
and bleated back at them with human plaintiveness.
I'm not the boy who crossed the North Sea,
standing watch, clinging to the bow
as the daylight slipped away and the signal lights
of passing ships came on the water.
I'm learning to do without the lordly Hudson
and the east branch of the lowly Delaware,
the frozen streams and the small mountain ponds
that come and go indifferently.
I'll work at it until all that remains is a hard-swept room
in a little house overlooking the Pacific,
until all that remains is the flat light and the drift,
the steady rocking of things in their places,
the tedium of Eden,
                                        the tedium of the Fall.

About the Author

Barry Seiler, a native of the Bronx, teaches at Rutgers University, Newark. He has a BA in English from Queens College in New York and an MFA in creative writing from the University of California at Irvine. He has published two previous books in the Akron Series in Poetry, *The Waters of Forgetting* and *Black Leaf.*

❄

About the Book

Frozen Falls was designed and typeset by Amy Petersen. The typeface, Minion, was designed by Robert Slimbach in 1990. *Frozen Falls* was printed on 60-pound Writers Natural and bound by McNaughton & Gunn of Saline, Michigan.